G IVEN THE SLOP that passed for dinner in England in those dark centuries before the advent of Gordon Ramsay et al., it is difficult to credit but nonetheless true that one of the animating prejudices of British life was a bias against food imported from France, a country whose contribution to cooking is roughly equal to Greece's early work on political philosophy. That was the background of the debate over the Corn Laws, which tightly controlled trade in what Americans call wheat, barley, and rye. It was a red-letter episode in the development of free-market thinking, with Walter Bagehot and the Manchester liberals defeating on every substantive point the protectionists, who were dominated by land-owning aristocrats – unlike the tragedy of *Richard III;* here Richmond and Buckingham were on the same side – cloaking their narrow, parochial self-interests with appeals to national security and patriotism. As often is the case in operational politics, winning the argument turned out to be worth precisely nothing: it took a famine to get Parliament to

liberalize the Corn Laws. Those familiar with that debate surely shake their heads sadly at the spectacle of Senator Marco Rubio of Florida, a bright young conservative light and Republican presidential contender who nestles too comfortably in the pocket of the sugar barons, arguing that U.S. sugar subsidies are a matter of national security. Without protectionist subsidies, he says, "other countries will capture the market share, our agricultural capacity will be developed into real estate … and then we lose the capacity to produce our own food, at which point we're at the mercy of a foreign country for food security." Richard Cobden and Lord Stanley weep.

Donald Trump smirks.

There is a profoundly illiberal tendency ascendant in American politics, and Donald Trump is its personification – not only anti-trade but venomously anti-immigrant, anti-commerce, nativist, populist, crude, and driven by anxiety. Trump is all those things and more. Trump is not – as far as the available evidence documents – a racist, but the

Donald Trump is poorly informed about immigration issues, and his policy proposals run from the ineffective to the fanciful.

movement he leads is, heavy as it is with Confederate revanchists willing to overlook Trump's impeccably Yankee credentials and white nationalists who complain that the Republican Party and the American conservative movement have been willing parties to what they call "race cuckoldry," a phrase with redolent sexual connotations that speak directly to the status anxiety at the heart of the Trump movement. Again, this is not to say that Trump is a racist – there is little indication that he harbors the sort of views that made David Duke a power in the same atavistic circles – or that all of his supporters, or even a majority of them, are racists. It is, however, impossible to separate the Trump movement from the racism and anti-Semitism that animate a nontrivial portion of its foot soldiers.

The question is rendered more complicated by the fact that there is a legitimate concern at the heart of Trump's populist appeal – and a legitimate foundation for the anxieties of his followers, including some of the detestable ones.

American institutions have failed, categorically, to address the problem of illegal immigration and in fact have gone so far as to studiously avoid even comprehending the question. The amnesty of 1986, agreed to by President Ronald Reagan, was sold as a prelude to the implementation of robust border-security measures, a classic case of politics on the "I'll gladly pay you Tuesday for a hamburger today" model. Millions more illegals crossed the border surreptitiously or entered legally and then overstayed the expiration of their visas. The official estimate is that there are some 11 million illegals residing in the

United States, but the reality is slightly more complicated than that, given that their U.S.-born children are legal under the practice of birthright citizenship – something Trump calls "stupid" and promises to end, though that is not actually within the scope of presidential power – while many of the pre-1986 illegals never sought to have their situation normalized. The question of legal status is an important one, but it is more fruitful to approach this as a question of tribal conflict. The 11 million (or more) illegals are one constituent of a larger community of unassimilated Hispanic immigrants who form a tribe apart, whose identities are shaped more by Mexican and Central American sympathies than by mainstream American culture, and who are to a very large extent present in the United States for merely economic reasons.

The familiar litany of complaints is no less true for being dear to the hearts of bigots. Hispanics have significantly higher rates of welfare dependency than whites ("Indicators of Welfare Dependence," U.S. Department of Health and Human Services), higher crime rates ("Crime in the United States 2013," Federal Bureau of Investigation), and lower levels of educational attainment (U.S. Census). Studies do show that immigrants as a category raise real wages for the native-born population, but this is statistical sleight of hand: the study generally cited in service of this claim (by Patricia Cortes of the University of Chicago) is slightly misleading in that the claim of higher real wages excludes the 15 percent of the population who are immigrants (thus the "native born" qualifier). When the entire population is considered, the effects of immigration on domestic wages are slightly negative. And the positive effects on real wages for the native-born population come almost exclusively through putting downward pressure on prices (which sends "real wages" higher even when the number on the paycheck is the same, or lower) by lowering wages at the labor-intensive, low-skilled end of the market.

Discussing these issues forthrightly from

a point of view of the American national interest is practically taboo.

The bipartisan consensus on the question of immigration is radically out of step with popular opinion (which typically runs about 70 or 80 percent in favor of stronger immigration controls) and reflects a nexus of political self-interest that is fundamentally corrupt. The Democrats believe, with good reason, that a growing Hispanic population means a growing Democratic base; Republicans, influenced partly by wishful thinking about their long-term prospects among Hispanic voters and partly by business interests that prefer a loosey-goosey immigration regime, have in their legislative efforts focused to a large extent on the less pressing question of normalizing the status of illegals currently residing in the United States and less on the much more pressing question of securing the border and getting control of visa enforcement.

Donald Trump is poorly informed about these issues, and his policy proposals run from the ineffective (concentrating our efforts on building a wall, when most new illegals do not enter by crossing the Mexican border) to the fanciful (coercing Mexico into paying for that wall). He is daft, bombastic, and inconsistent, having recently argued that the United States should consider permitting the resettlement of a large number of refugees displaced by the wars in the Middle East. (If your concern is assimilation, then compared with 100,000 Syrian Muslims, 100,000 Mexican farmworkers may as well have arrived

---

With four bankruptcies on its credit report thus far, Trump's casino empire has been in Chapter 11 more times than any other American business in the past 30 years.

---

on the *Mayflower*.) But Trump is not only willing to address the question from an American-interest point of view; he is also willing to do so belligerently. And to that he owes the remarkable measure of political success that he has enjoyed as of late September 2015.

*   *   *

He also owes more than a little something to his celebrity. Trump entered the race as the vessel of populist antiestablishment sentiment – the antithesis of former Florida Governor Jeb Bush, the presumptive favorite of the more moderate Chamber of Commerce wing of the Republican Party – but the early polls revealed a curious phenomenon. When a Fox News survey asked Republican primary voters to name a second-choice candidate, the surprising outcome was that among Trump voters, Bush was the most common second-choice pick, and among Bush voters, Trump was the most common second choice.

Bush, of course, is as close to the dead opposite of Trump as it is possible to be: the son of one Republican president and the brother of another, and an immigration dove who prides himself on regularly giving speeches and interviews in Spanish and who is married to a woman born in León, Mexico. (The latter fact, more than any other, drives Trump's white-nationalist supporters into a frenzy; the correspondence I have received from them on the matter of Mrs. Bush is detestable, enough to make one ashamed to be a member of not only the same race as these people but also the same species.) The Trump-Bush overlap in the early polls suggests that Trump's first foothold in the race was as much a question of celebrity – of simple name recognition – as anything else.

Trump's celebrity is of an odd sort. He is famous for being a wildly successful businessman, but it is not clear that he is any such thing. His career has, if anything, more closely resembled that of Paris Hilton, another heir to a splendid fortune who converted tawdry tabloid celebrity into a reality-television franchise, spinning that fame into a number of businesses that consist largely of renting her name to consumer-goods companies and entertainment venues.

With four bankruptcies on its credit report thus far, Trump's casino empire has been in Chapter 11 more times than any other American business in the past 30 years, according to CNN Money. Because Trump has relatively little involvement in publicly traded companies, his finances are opaque. He claims a personal net worth of about $10 billion, but *Forbes* — which has been tracking all things Trump for decades — puts the figure at half of that, and Bloomberg puts it at even less. Trump's actual money-in-the bank wealth (which is to say, cash and marketable equities) is about $300 million, which is, in real terms, less than the value of the vast real estate portfolio (comprising some 27,000 properties, mostly in the New York City area) left to him by his father, Fred Trump, the real author of the Trump fortune. S. V. Dáte, writing in

National Journal, calculates that if Trump had simply invested his share of the family business in a plain-vanilla S&P index fund in the early 1970s, when he was given control of what became the Trump Organization, he'd be as rich or richer than he is today. If he'd invested the $200 million net worth he claimed in the early 1980s similarly, Dáte calculates, he'd be worth substantially more than he is today, by billions of dollars.

But the story is slightly more complicated than that because, by Trump's own reckoning, his largest financial success has not been as a real estate developer (and certainly not as a casino operator) but as an entertainer. According to his financial filings, his single largest asset is not a building or golf course or resort but his "brand" – meaning the financial potency he believes is attached to his name – which he values at several billion dollars. But that brand is, by all indications, in rapid decline. NBC has confirmed that he will no longer be part of *The Apprentice* or *The*

Celebrity Apprentice, the reality-television shows that made his name and fortified his fortune; NBC and Univision are so disinclined to be associated with Trump that they are declining to broadcast the Miss USA pageant, which Trump owns. Macy's, which used to sell Trump-branded shirts and ties (Trump, the great advocate of economic nationalism, peddled garments made in Mexico and China) has discontinued its relationship with him. The value of a brand is in how much it can be licensed for, and it is not clear who, if anybody, wants the name *Trump* emblazoned on their products now – or who will in the future.

But if Trump has in fact ruined his brand, it isn't the first time he has ruined a business. Trump is very touchy about his bankruptcies and in fact insists from time to time that he has never been in bankruptcy, which is not exactly honest: he has never filed for bankruptcy under Chapter 7 or Chapter 13, the personal sections of the bankruptcy code, but has repeatedly taken recourse to Chapter 11, under which business bankruptcies are adjudicated. What this means is only that Trump has had the good sense to form corporations to shield his personal assets from the worst of his personal incompetence.

Just barely, though. His first bankruptcy, the 1991 reorganization of the Trump Taj Mahal casino, involved some $900 million of personal debt, which was more than four times what he'd claimed as his total net worth just nine years before. He'd claimed to be a billionaire in the late 1980s, but in 1990 *Forbes* dropped him from its billionaires list and estimated his net worth at around $500 million. For the next decade, press estimates of Trump's net worth are conspicuously sparse. The 1991 bankruptcy very nearly ruined him, and he was forced into a fire sale of assets, giving up a yacht, a small airline (Trump Shuttle), and much of his stake in the casino: he gave up 50 percent of the equity in the property to keep creditors at bay, and subsequent bankruptcies saw his stake reduced to 25 percent and then to 5 percent. The casino is expected to re-enter bankruptcy imminently, but given his diminished share in the company and his lack of control (he no longer even has a place on the board), we may charitably consider future Taj Mahal bankruptcies to be Trump in name only.

Many entrepreneurs hit bumps in the road, but it is far from clear that Trump has in fact come roaring back: Timothy O'Brien's 2005 book *TrumpNation* put the developer's net worth at $250 million or less. Trump sued for defamation, and he lost. During the lawsuit, documents were produced from the gimlet-eyed underwriters at Deutsche Bank, who were at the time considering lending Trump money for a project in Chicago, and they estimated his net worth at less than $1 billion. They made him the loan anyway and came to regret it. Trump defaulted on the loan, and they were forced to sue him for the debt.

Trump's performance in the real estate business is, then, open to question. But his performance in the business of being a celebrity has been, without question, impressive. Despite his substantial inherited wealth, Trump was a little-known figure even in his native New York City until 1973, when he and his father and their organization were accused of discriminating against black applicants in their capacity as apartment landlords and were sued under the Fair Housing Act of 1968. The charges were serious – that the Trump firm had insisted on different terms and conditions when applicants were black and that it had gone so far as to lie to black applicants about the availability of rentals. Trump's response was his by-now-familiar pattern: bluster (calling the charges "absolutely ridiculous"), litigation (he filed a $100 million lawsuit against the government), and then quietly reaching a settlement. Trump insisted that the issue was never race but about his being forced to accept renters who were on welfare. Nonetheless, he agreed to monitoring by the Urban League.

Trump knuckled under in the end, but the discrimination lawsuit made him famous. Shortly after the settlement, the *New York*

Times was profiling him in risibly fawning terms: "He looks ever so much like Robert Redford. He rides around town in a chauffeured silver Cadillac with his initials, DJT,

---

Trump came to adopt the view that there is no such thing as bad publicity: he was mainly known to the world as a tabloid cretin for many years.

---

on the plates. He dates slinky fashion models, belongs to the most elegant clubs and, at only 30 years of age, estimates that he is worth 'more than $200 million.'" Ever so much of a muchness. Trump would soon come to adopt the view that there is no such thing as bad publicity: he was mainly known to the world as a tabloid cretin for many years, with his high-profile divorce from Ivana Trump, his affair with Marla Maples (who, like Trump, would go so far as to participate in professional wrestling events in the service of furthering her celebrity), the bankruptcies, the rivalry with Merv Griffin, and the inevitable lawsuits between them. The fantastic tackiness of his style, epitomized by the gold-plated seat-belt buckles on his personal airplane, is the stuff of legend. When the producers of *The Devil's Advocate*, a cheesy Al Pacino vehicle in part about a despicable New York City billionaire real estate developer who is guilty of a multiple murder (and, it is suggested, a quasi-incestuous pedophiliac affair with his stepdaughter), they must have been shocked at their good fortune when Trump allowed them to use his apartment, with its gilt moldings, imitation frescoes, and faux-rococo furnishings as a set. Trump was the butt of the joke, but that's showbiz.

And showbiz is very much what the Donald Trump presidential campaign is all about.

* * *

As of this writing, the only item under "Positions" on the Donald J. Trump for President website is "Immigration Reform," and the entry therein replicated a "policy paper" – it doesn't quite live up to that billing – issued by Team Trump with great fanfare in August. Though the paper did garner some qualified praise, including from an editorial in my magazine, *National Review*, there is not a great deal to it, and much of what is there is defective. Talk-radio commentators celebrated the paper's opening section, which contains no policy proposals at all but is instead merely a selection of three slogans, all of which have been part of the ordinary discourse surrounding immigration reform for years: "1. A nation without borders is not a nation." "2. A nation without laws is not a nation." "3. A nation that does not serve its own citizens is not a nation." From this three largely unexceptional policy prescriptions are decocted: "There must be a wall across the southern border." "Laws passed in accordance with our Constitutional system of government must be enforced."

"Any immigration plan must improve jobs, wages, and security for all Americans." Though the idea of a point-to-point wall on the border stretching uninterrupted from Las Palomas Wildlife Management Area on the Gulf of Mexico in Texas to Border Field State Park on the Pacific Ocean in California is a logistical impossibility (it would require, among other things, building a wall atop several substantial bodies of water, including the Rio Grande and the 65,000-acre Amistad Reservoir, to say nothing of steep canyons and other obstacles, and expropriating enormous amount of privately owned land along the border), the prospect of building barriers in the border zone is something that enjoys broad support. You would be hard-pressed to find a candidate anywhere on the ideological spectrum, from Ted Cruz to Bernie Sanders, who argues for categorically declining to enforce the law or who objects to the notion that immigration law ought to serve the economic interests of Americans. Likewise, there is no candidate who objects to the three slogans at the heart of Trump's proposal. Shallow talk-radio rhetoric notwithstanding, there is not an open-borders candidate in the race, and no movement is afoot to abolish borders or to make the United States a nation without law. There is, however, a great deal of disagreement about how best to go about policing immigration and how to prioritize the various interests involved, which are, inevitably, in competition with one another.

Trump's proposal – more of a posture, in truth – that Mexico be made to pay for the wall is so silly as to hardly deserve being addressed. Trump holds out the threat of cutting off foreign aid to Mexico as a cudgel with which to beat the Mexicans into submission, but U.S. foreign aid to Mexico is trivial, and it amounts to barely a rounding error on remittances sent from Mexican nationals in the United States home to family in Mexico. With that in mind, Trump threatens to put a levy on the wages of Mexicans working illegally in the United States and fund the wall with the proceeds. This would

Trump's go-to position is that the United States faces the problems that it faces because its leadership is "stupid" — stupid here mainly meaning "not Donald Trump."

require unprecedented surveillance of effectively all individual Americans' banking activity and transfers and presumes a body of knowledge – the source and recipients of illegal wages – that does not exist. Indeed, if the U.S. government had at its disposal that sort of information about wages being paid illegally to illegal aliens, it could simply intervene directly in the workplace and solve almost the entirety of the illegal-immigration problem at one go.

A Mexico-funded wall is a simple solution, and, like most simple solutions, it isn't a solution at all. In fact, most of the illegals coming to the United States now are not Mexicans. (They are mainly Central Americans, but there are significant illegal populations from Ireland, Eastern Europe, Africa, Asia, the Middle East, and indeed from almost every corner of the world.) What presents even more of a problem is that while millions may have walked or swum across the border from Mexico over the decades, the majority of illegals enter the country now through airports and other legal points of entry. Border hoppers are a minority of the new illegals; the majority today enter legally on visas and simply refuse to go home when their legal presence in the United States comes to an end.

Tracking the population of visa overstayers presents an enormously complex logistical problem, one that is significantly complicated by longstanding legal protections and social norms regarding privacy in the United States. As any Western visitor to India or China can tell you, it is not uncommon for foreigners to be asked to show their passports and visas when doing ordinary things such as checking into a hotel or traveling within those countries. Our Asian friends are a little less queasy about racial profiling than we are, and if your blond hair, blue eyes, or foreign accent flags you as a likely foreigner in Beijing or Bangalore, you can expect to be treated as one until you prove that you aren't. It is difficult to imagine a legal reform – to say nothing of a radical revolution in social norms – that would result in the clerk at the desk in a Holiday Inn or a Hertz car rental demanding satisfaction that your papers are in order before you are permitted to check in or transact your business. And given that illegals who overstay their visas have the option, even during the reign of plastic, to live in a cash-only economy, to travel within the United States by exclusively private conveyance, to forgo renting apartments in their own names, etc., policing overstays is going to be a very, very challenging project, one that requires a great deal of investment and expenditure of energy on the part of governmental authorities that are not, if experience is any guide, much inclined to exert themselves. In the aftermath of the terrorist attacks of Sept. 11, 2001, we fought two wars in response to an incident that could have been prevented by competent visa controls.

The Trump element is not much inclined to consider policy problems at that granular level. If that's obvious in the case of immigration – Trump's keynote issue – it is even more so in his other area of acute concern: trade.

* * *

Trump's go-to position is that the United States faces the problems that it faces because its leadership is "stupid" – *stupid* here mainly meaning "not Donald Trump" – which allows Americans to be exploited by wicked foreigners. In Trump's mind, the millions who have come to the United States from Mexico and Central America are not desperately poor people fleeing dysfunctional societies and oppressive governments but rather pawns in a plot hatched in Mexico City to flood the

United States with criminals – "rapists," in his famous insistence, another bit of that characteristic sexual panic at the heart of Trumpism. Meanwhile, U.S. trade deficits and the disruptive effects of globalization are not natural outgrowths of technological change, specialization, and comparative advantage, but rather are the result of scheming, mainly in Beijing but also in Mexico City. Trump's trade platform is, essentially, to negotiate good deals instead of bad deals, a proposal that he forwards with something that seems very much like the earnest conviction that this never has occurred to anybody else.

There is an undeniable ethnic angle to the trade paranoia ascendant in American politics – not only with Trump and his camp but also with left-wing antitraders such as Bernie Sanders. If you listen to the speeches of the antitraders, you'd think that our trade deficits are exclusively with poor brown people in sweaty climes: Trump with his wily Chinese and nefarious Mexicans, Sanders with his categorically inscrutable Asians from Bombay to Beijing. The United States in fact runs substantial trade deficits with Germany and Canada, two very white and high-wage countries, and U.S. manufacturers compete more directly with Canadian and German firms than they do with those in China. The business of sewing together cheap sneakers and assembling inexpensive plastic toys was moribund in the United States long before China's rise from famine to mere poverty. Estimates vary significantly, but CNN's interpretation of International Labor Organization data puts the median monthly paycheck of a private-sector worker in China at less than $400 a month, while other estimates run closer to $700. Which is to say, the ingenious negotiators in Beijing have conspired to keep Chinese consumers from enjoying the bounty of high-value-added American manufacturing by keeping them poor. Until the shale-oil renaissance, a very large portion (the majority in some years) of the U.S. trade deficit consisted of oil imports. That the U.S. balance of trade in petroleum would be in permanent deficit is inevitable, given the fact that the U.S. government in 1975, gripped by Trumpkin antitrade thinking, banned the export of crude oil. "We'll teach those dirty foreigners a lesson by . . . not taking their money!"

Trump and his movement abominate the North American Free Trade Agreement as a job killer and a shackle on U.S. prosperity, a position that is not borne out by the economic data. The actual economic scholarship suggests that NAFTA has had a modest positive effect on U.S. employment and a much more strongly positive effect (indeed, much stronger than anticipated) on the U.S. services

Trump and his movement abominate NAFTA as a job killer and a shackle on U.S. prosperity, a position that is not borne out by the economic data.

sector, particularly financial services. In real terms (which is to say, in inflation-adjusted terms), U.S. manufacturing output, which had been climbing substantially before NAFTA, continued climbing afterward – and climbs still. Manufacturing output is, in fact, nearly 70 percent higher today than it was when NAFTA was passed. It is the case that manufacturing makes up a smaller share of U.S. economic output today than it did in, say, 1970, but that is not the result of a decline in manufacturing – no such decline has happened – but rather a result of the fact that other sectors of the economy have grown even quicker. There was, practically speaking, no meaningful information-technology sector in 1955, and the modern American financial-services industry would be entirely unrecognizable to a time traveler from the 1960s.

The antitrade hysteria is not the result of a crisis in American manufacturing; it is the result of a crisis in American manhood.

* * *

The intersection of authoritarian politics with homoeroticism is a subject of some historical interest, from the Nazi enthusiasm for the sculptures of Josef Thorak and Arno Breker to the Italian Futurists' ritual rejection of all things feminine. That mostly petered out around the time Francisco Franco stopped rocking that fur in official portraiture, though it has made occasional ignominious appearances in Democratic politics too. But the combination of homoerotic fascination and gay panic that marks the Trump movement is truly remarkable, something unseen in American politics.

It is the result of a confluence of unhappy developments. There exist a number of literatures (to use the term charitably) dedicated to servicing the grievances of socially and sexually disappointed men. The men's-rights movement, like the Trump movement, flits occasionally upon a genuine grievance (e.g., the radically unequal treatment of men and women in divorce and custody law) but is more generally oriented toward wallowing.

Its adjunct, the "game" community, provides advice to would-be pickup artists, its fundamental structure being the divide between "alpha" and "beta" males, and its goal being the development of pseudoscientific strategies for the latter to impersonate the former. The so-called human-biodiversity community seizes upon and twists the work of scholars such as Charles Murray to develop racial theories of, well, *everything*; the border between the biodiversity enthusiasts and the outright racism of the white-nationalist community (the leading online journal of which has, unsurprisingly, endorsed Donald Trump for president) is porous.

The ruling common metaphors in these cracked alternate realities are the alpha-beta distinction and cuckoldry, which is, curiously enough, rarely discussed in its traditional sense. The precise number of American men who are unknowingly raising children who are not their own is a matter of some dispute; among those suspicious enough to request paternity tests, some 30 percent (!) discover that they are not the father of the child in question, according to the *New York Times*. It is therefore not entirely surprising that among Trump's admirers we find a substantial population of purportedly heterosexual men who praise their candidate in extravagantly gonadal terms – I will not here bother to catalog the examples of scrotal and penile celebration I have encountered in my desultory correspondence with the Trumpkins – while Trump's critics are ritually denounced as beta males, "cucks," or, in the popular white-nationalist phrase, "cuckservatives." The *cuckservative* appellation has its origins in anti-Semitic tropes ("neocons cucking for Israel"), though it occurs now with the most frequency and greatest ferocity in the realm of race, especially concerning anxieties about the diminution of the white majority in the United States.

One has to respect Trump as a thespian: he is, after all, the Little Lord Fauntleroy of Fifth Avenue, a coddled product of the bottom end of the Ivy League, a draft dodger, and a man whose idea of kinetic adventure is golf. That lion-hunting dentist that the world was so mad at is Ernest Hemingway next to Trump.

But one can see the fantasy appeal, especially for a socially (sexually, economically) disappointed member of the downwardly mobile classes. American men born in the 1960s, '70s, or '80s hark back to an imaginary blue-collar economy in which a man could earn a secure place in society (and hence in the sexual hierarchy) through simple dedicated labor at a factory. The workingman's paradise of the postwar era has been romanticized to the point of fiction, but it is a powerful fiction. By some estimates, the median real wage of the male American worker peaked in approximately 1973 as a highly unusual condition of the immediate postwar economy. (The savagery of the war had left the United States practically alone unscathed among the major industry powers, producing a temporary hegemony that was destined to be short-lived.) Household incomes increased mainly as a result of the entrance of more women into the workforce. Despite the prominence of military engagements in recent American history, traditional male virtues such as assertive physical courage are mocked and even pathologized in mainstream white communities even as they remain potent social forces in the poor minority communities where the Walter Mittys of the Trumpkin tendency dare not go. The decline of marriage means that there is no real respite from the endless competition for social status. And in what must surely be most galling for these unfortunates, the people who are making the best money and winning the highest status in the globalized economy are the ones who care the least about immigration controls, who are the least likely to have a robust white identity of any sort, and who are not troubled at all by Spanish-language billboards (found in neighborhoods they seldom pass through). Somebody must be blamed: the Chinese, the Mexicans, the Jews.

Above all, the Republicans. Trump is seeking to be the Republican Party's headliner;

the Trumpkins are seeking to be its *end*. Here, the conservative movement has been its own worst enemy. The left is justified in its schadenfreude as the perpetual-rage machine – created by Fox News personalities, talk radio,

---

Trump is the Little Lord Fauntleroy of Fifth Avenue, a coddled product of the bottom end of the Ivy League, a draft dodger, and a man whose idea of kinetic adventure is golf.

---

the less intellectually rigorous websites and journals, and the angry right-wing mobs on Twitter and Facebook – turns its attention not to Barack Obama and his epigones, but to the Republican congressional leadership he has so deftly outmaneuvered, the (largely imaginary) "donor class" that allegedly dominates

Republican affairs, the Chamber of Commerce, and Fox News. The case of Megyn Kelly is particularly amusing, as the famously sexy television personality displays the unforgivable temerity to respond to Donald Trump's lumpy version of alpha masculinity with derision. One gets the feeling that most of the Trumpkins sending enraged online missives in the direction of Kelly were typing with one hand. The permanently outraged populist right, endlessly rehearsing the tragedy of the wicked establishment's eternal betrayal of the holy base, is almost exclusively a creation of the entertainment wing of the conservative movement, and it is satisfyingly ironic to see Dr. Frankenstein's monster finally turn its inchoate rage on its creator. (For here there is no Bride of Frankenstein.) Roger Ailes's feud with Donald Trump has something of the professional-wrestling beef about it: this is his circus, and these are his monkeys.

* * *

It is impossible to say how and when the Trump phenomenon will end. It should end; rather, it never should have begun. Donald J. Trump spent most of his life as a progressive Democrat, a patron of Charles Schumer, Nancy Pelosi, and Hillary Rodham Clinton – the woman against whom Trump presumably would be running. He is a lifelong crony capitalist who boasts of using his wealth to buy political favors to make himself wealthier still. He is a proponent of the thieving *Kelo* eminent-domain regime and has attempted to suborn local governments into using eminent domain to seize properties in order to clear the way for his casino developments. He was until the day before yesterday as absolutist a proabortion advocate as any you'd find at an Emily's List meeting. He has proposed daft, confiscatory wealth taxes and remains in accord with Warren Buffett and Elizabeth Warren on taxation. His views on trade and immigration are much more like those of Bernie Sanders, the Vermont socialist, than they are anything that might plausibly be

> *Trump is seeking to be the Republican Party's headliner; the Trumpkins are seeking to be its end.*

described as "conservative" in the American context. He is apparently incapable of stringing together three complete English sentences, lies reflexively and instinctively, and contradicts his own pronouncements at every turn. On the verge of his 70th birthday, his mind remains unsettled about the most elementary issues of our time.

But he is rich. He is famous. He has the power of celebrity and a true demagogue's gift for dipping his snout into the very worst tendencies of our politics, the same illiberal tendencies that had 19th century Englishmen turning up their noses at French wheat even as famine was at their door. He would have us turn away from trade and indeed turn away from the world and its complexities, imagining ourselves to be safe behind our wall. That's a high price to pay for an immigration platform that is exceeded by the platforms of many other Republican candidates in every way except in the quantity of bile in which it is soaked. But the bile is the attraction here, not the policy.

Donald J. Trump's admirers gleefully consider the possibility that he could be the end of the Republican Party. He could be the end of a lot more than that.

First American edition published in 2015 by Encounter Books,
an activity of Encounter for Culture and Education, Inc.,
a nonprofit, tax exempt corporation.
Encounter Books website address: www.encounterbooks.com

Manufactured in the United States and printed on
acid-free paper. The paper used in this publication meets
the minimum requirements of ANSI/NISO Z39.48-1992
(R 1997) (*Permanence of Paper*).

FIRST AMERICAN EDITION

LIBRARY OF CONGRESS
CATALOGING-IN-PUBLICATION DATA
IS AVAILABLE

Williamson, Kevin D.
The case against Trump / Kevin D. Williamson.
pages   cm. — (Encounter broadsides ; 46)
ISBN 978-1-59403-877-8 (pbk. : alk. paper) —
ISBN 978-1-59403-878-5 (ebook)

10 9 8 7 6 5 4 3 2 1

SERIES DESIGN BY CARL W. SCARBROUGH